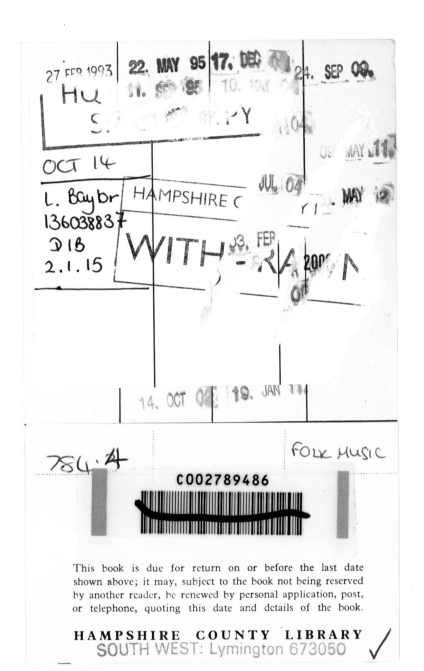

THE FOLK MUSIC ANTHOLOGY
'MR. TAMBOURINE MAN'

MR TAMBOURINE MAN

WORDS & MUSIC BY BOB DYLAN

jin-gle jan - gle morn-in' I'll come fol - low-in' you.

5th time Fine

Verse

1. Though I know that eve-nin's em - pire has re-turned in - to sand,

Van-ished from my hand, Left me blind-ly here to stand but still not

sleep-in'! My wea-ri-ness a - maz-es me I'm

brand - ed on my feet. I have no one to meet And the

Repeat 3 times

an - cient emp - ty street's too dead for dream-in'. _____

Refrain:

Verse 2. Take me on a trip upon your magic swirlin' ship
My senses have been stripped, my hands can't feel to grip
My toes too numb to step, wait only for my boot heels
To be wanderin'
I'm ready to go anywhere, I'm ready for to fade
Into my own parade, cast your dancin' spell my way
I promise to go under it.

Refrain:

Verse 3. Though you might hear laughin' spinnin' swingin' madly across the sun
It's not aimed at anyone, it's just escapin' on the run
And but for the sky there are no fences facin'
And if you hear vague traces of skippin' reels of rhyme
To your tambourine in time, it's just a ragged clown behind
I wouldn't pay it any mind, it's just a shadow you're
Seein' that he's chasin'.

Refrain:

Verse 4. Then take me disappearin' through the smoke rings of my mind
Down the foggy ruins of time, far past the frozen leaves
The haunted, frightened trees out to the windy beach
Far from the twisted reach of crazy sorrow
Yes, to dance beneath the diamond sky with one hand wavin' free
Silhouetted by the sea, circled by the circus sands
With all memory and fate driven deep beneath the waves
Let me forget about today until tomorrow.

Refrain:

BEFORE THE DELUGE

WORDS & MUSIC BY JACKSON BROWNE

Some of them were dream - ers ___
Some of them knew pleas - ure ___
Some of them were an - gry ___ at the

and some of them_ were fools ___ who were mak - ing plans___ and
and some of them_ knew pain, ___ and for some of them___ it was
way the earth was a - bused ___ by the men who learned_ how to

by and by, _____

when the light ____ that's lost with - in us reach - es the sky. __

D.S. % (no repeats) al Coda

To Coda

Coda

Repeat and fade

SONG FOR THE ASKING

WORDS & MUSIC BY PAUL SIMON

wait - ing ___ all my ___ life. ___

Think-ing it o-ver, I've been sad, ___ Think-ing it o-ver, I'd be more than glad To

change my ways ___ for the ask - ing, Ask me and I ___ will

play All the love that I ___ hold in - side.

TAKE ME HOME, COUNTRY ROADS

WORDS & MUSIC BY BILL DANOFF, TAFFY NIVERT & JOHN DENVER

younger than the mountains, growin' like a breeze.
misty taste of moonshine, teardrop in my eye.

Country Roads, take me home to the

place I belong: West Virginia,

mountain momma, Take me home, Country

Roads.   All my   I hear her voice, in the

morn - in' hour she calls___ me, the ra - di - o re - minds me of my

home far a - way, and driv - in' down the road I get a feel - in' that I

should have been home yes - ter - day,___ yes - ter - day.___

D.S. %̸ al ⊕ Coda

Coda

Roads,_____ take_ me home,_____ Coun - try Roads,_____

___ take_ me home,_____ Coun - try Roads._____

LUKA

WORDS & MUSIC BY SUZANNE VEGA

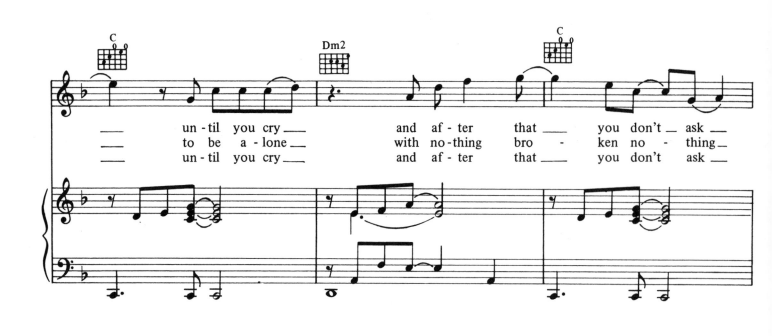

un-til you cry ___ and af-ter that ___ you don't ___ ask ___
to be a-lone ___ with no-thing bro - ken no - thing ___
un-til you cry ___ and af-ter that ___ you don't ___ ask ___

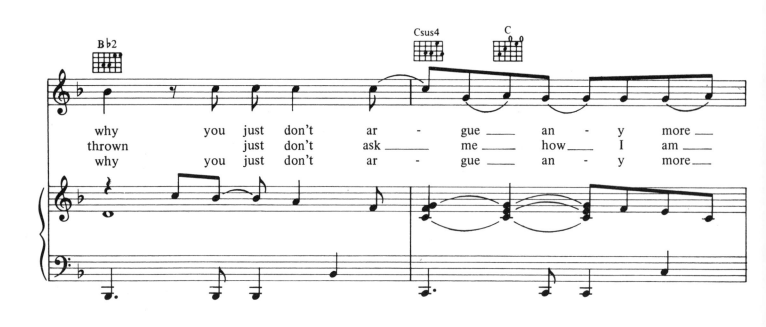

why you just don't ar - gue ___ an - y more ___
thrown just don't ask ___ me ___ how ___ I am ___
why you just don't ar - gue ___ an - y more ___

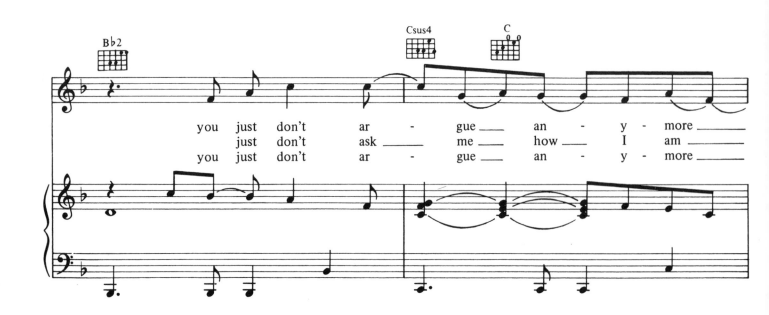

you just don't ar - gue ___ an - y - more ___
just don't ask ___ me ___ how ___ I am ___
you just don't ar - gue ___ an - y - more ___

you just don't ar - gue an - y - more.
just don't ask
you just don't ar - gue an - y - more.

me how I am.

me what it was.

APRIL COME SHE WILL

WORDS & MUSIC BY PAUL SIMON

SAD LISA

WORDS & MUSIC BY CAT STEVENS

must
near
see

be._____
me._____
her._____

Li- sa, Li- sa_____ sad Li- sa, Li- sa._____

1.2.3.

2. Her
3. (Instrumental)
4. She

4.

HOMEWARD BOUND

WORDS & MUSIC BY PAUL SIMON

1. I'm sit - tin' in the rail - way sta - tion, got a tick - et for my
2. Ev - 'ry day's an end - less stream of cig - a - rettes and
(3. To -) night I'll sing my songs a - gain, I'll play the game

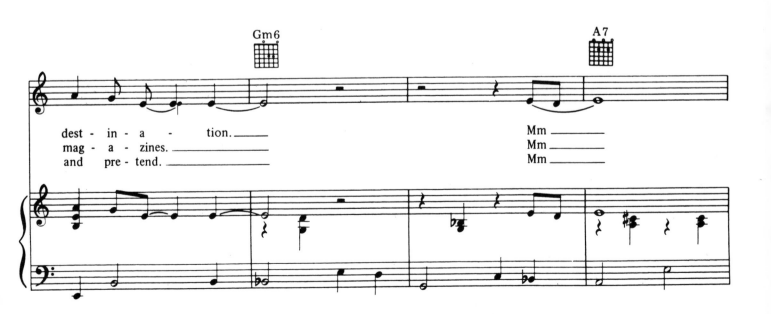

dest - in - a - tion. Mm
mag - a - zines. Mm
and pre - tend. Mm

Dm   Bb

And   On   a   tour___ of   one night stands my suit - case and gui - tar
But   each town looks___ the   same to me, the mov - ies and the fac-

C

in hand___   and ev - 'ry   stop is   neat - ly planned___ for   a
- tor - ies___   and ev - 'ry strang - er's face I   see___   re-
- ri - ty___   like emp - ti - ness   in   har - mon - ny___   I

G7   C

po - et   and   a   one_____ man   band._____
minds me   that   I long_____ to   be,_____
need some - one   to com - fort me._____

Chorus:

C   F   C

Home - ward___ Bound,   I   wish I   was,_____

f

28

RIBBON OF DARKNESS

WORDS & MUSIC BY GORDON LIGHTFOOT

Bridge:

3. Rain is fall -ing on the mead - ow___ Where once my love and I did lie, ___ Now she is gone from the mead - ow, ___ My love, good - bye. ___ me. ___

Dal %

(to Refrain 4)

2. Refrain

Clouds a gath'rin' o'er my head
That kill the day and hide the sun,
That shroud the night when day is done,
Ribbon of darkness over me.

(To Bridge 3.)

4. Refrain

Ribbon of darkness over me,
Where once the world was young as spring,
Where flow'rs did bloom and birds did sing,
Ribbon of darkness over me.

(To Bridge 5.)

5. Bridge

Here in this cold room lying
Don't want to see no one but you,
Lord, I wish I could be dying
To forget you.

(To Refrain 6.)

6. Refrain

Oh how I wish your heart could see
How mine just aches and breaks all day,
Come on home and take away
This ribbon of darkness over me.

(Finis)

ONE DAY AT A TIME

WORDS & MUSIC BY MARIJOHN WILKIN & KRIS KRISTOFFERSON

ask - ing from you. _____ Just give me the strength to do ev - 'ry - day what I have to do. _____ Yes - ter - day's gone, _____ sweet Je - sus, _____ and to - mor - row may nev - er be mine. _____

34

2. Do you remember when you walked among men
   Well, Jesus, you know if you're looking below that it's worse now than then
   Pushin' and shovin', crowding my mind
   So for my sake, Lord, teach me to take ONE DAY AT A TIME.

AT SEVENTEEN

WORDS & MUSIC BY JANIS IAN

Moderately

I learned the truth at sev - en - teen__ that love was meant for beau-
(A) brown - eyed girl in hand - me downs__ whose name I nev - er could
(To) those of us who know__ the pain__ of val - en - tines that nev -

- ty queens__ And high school girls — with clear - skinned smiles__ who
— pro - nounce,__ said, "Pit - y, please,__ the ones__ who serve,__ they
- er came,__ and those whose names__ were nev - er called__ when

mar - ried young and then — re - tired. — The
on - ly get what they — de - serve." — The
choos - ing sides for bas - ket - ball. — It was

val - en - tines I nev - er knew, — the Fri - day night cha - rades —
rich re - la - tioned home - town queen — Mar - ries in - to what —
long a - go and far — a - way, — the world was young - er than —

— of youth — Were spent on one — more beau - ti - ful, — At
— she needs: — A guar - an - tee — of com - pa - ny — And
— to - day, — And dreams were all — they gave — for free — to

37

sev - en - teen, I learned the truth.___
ha - ven for the eld - er - ly.___
ug - ly duck - ling girls ___ like me.___

And
Re -
We all

those of us ___ with rav - aged fac - es,
mem - ber those ___ who win ___ the game ___
___ play the game ___ and when ___ we dare ___

lack - ing in the so -
lose the love ___ they sought ___
to cheat our - selves ___ at sol -

- cial grac - es,
- to gain ___
- i - taire ___

Des - p'rate - ly ___ re - mained ___ at home ___ in -
In de - ben - tures ___ of qual - i - ty ___ and
In - vent - ing lov - ers on ___ the phone, ___ re -

SO LONG MARIANNE

WORDS & MUSIC BY LEONARD COHEN

I was some sort of gyp-sy boy, — before I let you take me home; — so long, Ma - ri - anne, — it's time that we be-gan to laugh and cry and

Chorus
Now,

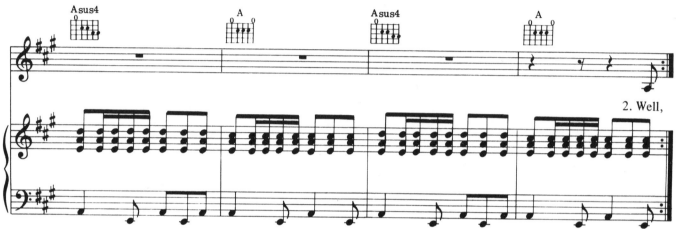

2. Well,

Come over to the window my little darling
I'd like to try to read your palm
I used to think I was some sort of gypsy boy
Before I let you take me home.

CHORUS:
So long, Marianne, it's time that we began
To laugh and cry and laugh about it all again.

Well, you know that I love to live with you
But you make me forget so very much
I forget to pray for the angel
And then the angels forget to pray for us.

We met when we were almost young
Deep in the green lilac park
You held on to me like I was a crucifix
As we went kneeling through the dark.

Your letters they all say that you're beside
    me now
Then why do I feel alone?
I'm standing on a ledge and your fine
    spider web
Is fastening my ankle to a stone.

For now I need your hidden love
I'm cold as a new razor blade
You left when I told you I was curious
I never said that I was brave.

Oh, you are really such a pretty one
I see you've gone and changed your
    name again
And just when I climbed this whole
    mountainside
To wash my eyelids in the rain.

O your eyes, well, I forget your eyes
Your body's at home in every sea
How come you gave away your news
    to everyone
That you said was a secret for me.

42

LONG AGO AND FAR AWAY

WORDS & MUSIC BY JAMES TAYLOR

44

can-not stand the cold. And in be-tween what might

have been and what has come to pass, a

mis-be-got-ten guess, a-las, and bits of bro-ken glass.

Where do your gold-en rain-bows end?

47

ON THE BORDER

WORDS & MUSIC BY AL STEWART

The fish-ing boats_ go out a-cross_ the eve-ning wa - ter,

smug-gling guns_ and arms_ a-cross_ the Span-ish bor - der.

The wind whips up the waves_ so loud;_ the ghost moon sails a-

mong the clouds___ and turns the ri - fles in - to sil - ver

on the bor - der.

On my wall___ the col-ours of the maps___ are run - ning. From
Late last night___ the rain was knock-ing on___ my win - dow. I

Af - ri - ca___ the winds,___ they talk of chang - es com - ing. The
moved a - cross___ the dark - ened room, and in___ the lamp-glow I

torch-es flare up in ____ the night.__ The hand that sets the farms ___ a - light_ has

thought I saw down in ____ the street _ the spir - it of the cen - tu - ry__

spread the word_ to those _ who're wait-ing on the bor - der.

tell - ing us_ that we're_ all stand-ing on the bor - der.

In the vil - lage where I grew_ up

In the is - lands where I grew_ up

noth-ing seems the same.__ Still you nev - er see the change_ from day_ to day.__

noth-ing seems the same.__ It's just the pat-terns that re - main,_ an emp - ty shell.__

No one no - tic - es the cus - toms   slip a - way.
But there's a   strange - ness in the air__ you   feel too well.

1.

2. *D. S. % al Coda*

The

Repeat and fade

Coda

in - to sil - ver   on the bor - der,

Repeat and fade

on the bor - der.

EARLY MORNIN' RAIN

WORDS & MUSIC BY GORDON LIGHTFOOT

1. In the ear - ly morn - in' rain _____

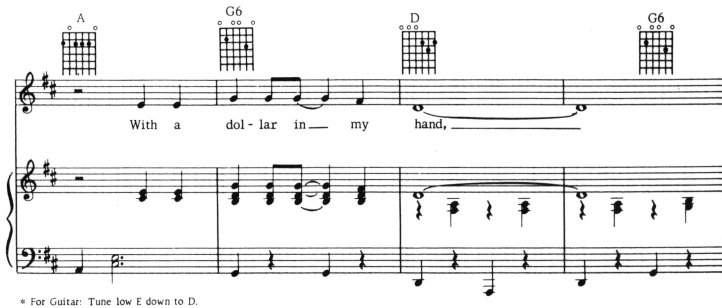

With a dol - lar in ___ my hand, _____

* For Guitar: Tune low E down to D.

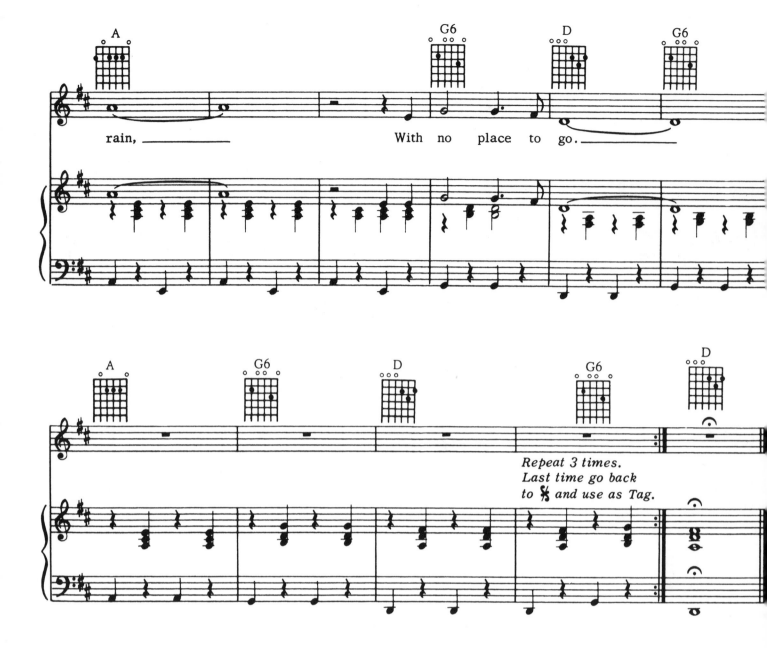

2. Out on runway number nine
   Big seven-o-seven set to go,
   But I'm stuck here in the grass
   Where the cold wind blows.
   Now the liquor tasted good,
   And the women all were fast,
   Well, there she goes, my friend,
   She's rollin' now at last.

3. Hear the mighty engines roar,
   See the silver bird on high,
   She's away and westward bound,
   Far above the clouds she'll fly,
   Where the mornin' rain don't fall,
   And the sun always shines,
   She'll be flyin' o'er my home
   In about three hours time.

4. This old airport's got me down,
   It's no earthly good to me,
   'Cause I'm stuck here on the ground
   As cold and drunk as I can be.
 * You can't jump a jet plane
   Like you can a freight train,
   So I'd best be on my way
   In the early mornin' rain.

 * Repeat from here for Tag. (instrumental only)

54

JESSE

WORDS & MUSIC BY JANIS IAN

Jes - se,___ come home,___ there is a hole___ in the bed where we slept___

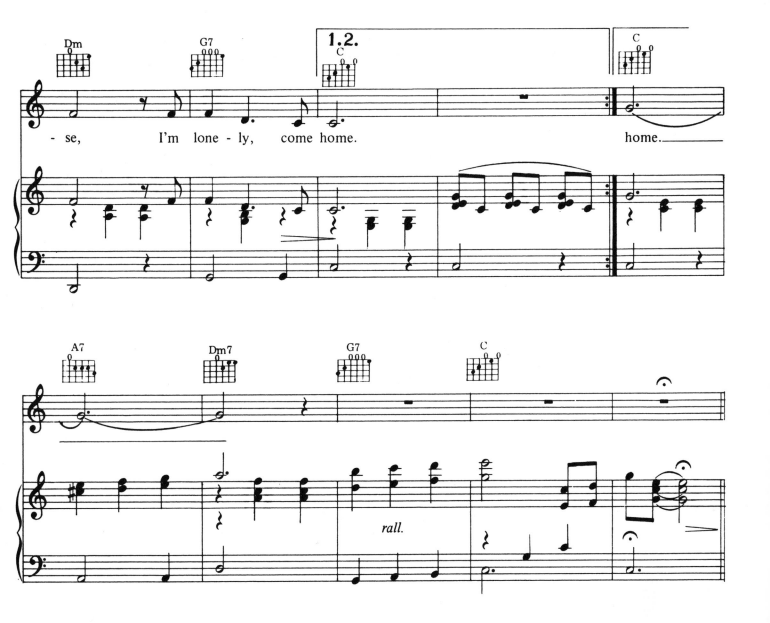

2. Jesse the floors and the paths recalling your steps
   And I remember too,
   All the pictures are fading and shading grey,
   But I still set a place on the table at noon
   And I'm leaving the light on the stairs,
   No, I'm not scared, I'll wait for you
   Oh Jesse, I'm lonely, come home.

3. Jesse, the 'spread on the bed
   Is like when you left, I've kept it up for you.
   And all the blues and the greens have been recently cleaned,
   And it's seemingly new - hey Jesse me and you.
   We'll swallow the light on the stairs
   We'll do up my hair and sleep unaware
   Hey, Jesse, I'm lonely, come home.

OPERATOR (THAT'S NOT THE WAY IT FEELS)

WORDS & MUSIC BY JIM CROCE

59

2. Operator, could you help me place this call?
   'Cause I can't read the number that you just gave me
   There's something in my eyes,
   You know it happens every time;
   I think about the love that I thought would save me.

   (Chorus)

3. Operator, let's forget about this call,
   There's no one there I really wanted to talk to.
   Thank you for your time,
   'Cause you've been so much more than kind
   And you can keep the dime.

   (Chorus)

ONLY LOVE CAN BREAK YOUR HEART

WORDS & MUSIC BY NEIL YOUNG

CRACKING

WORDS & MUSIC BY SUZANNE VEGA

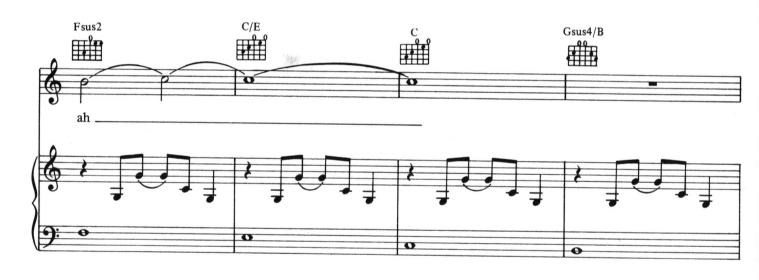

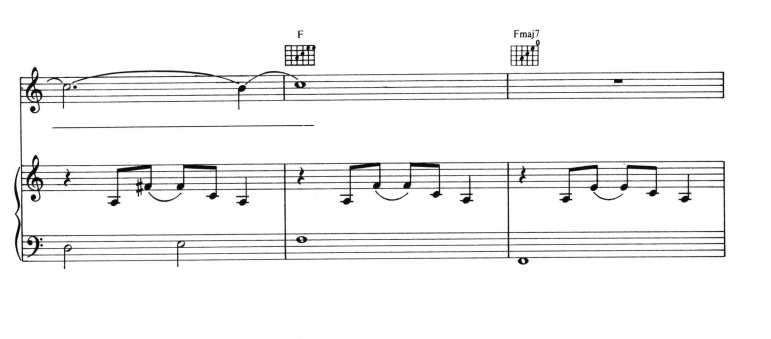

It's a one time thing it just
My heart is bro - ken

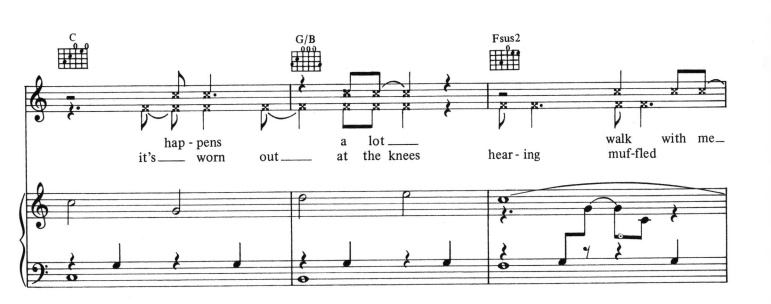

hap - pens a lot
it's worn out at the knees

walk with me
hear - ing muf-fled

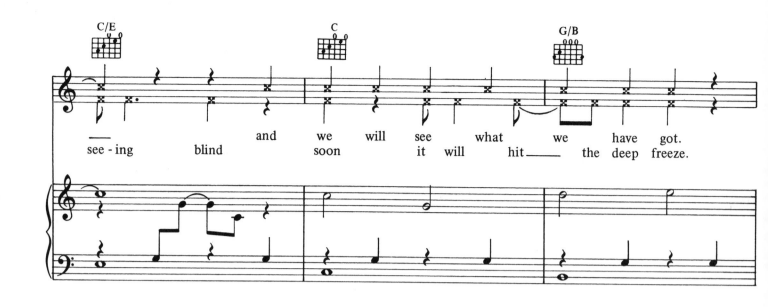

see-ing blind and we will see what we have got.
soon it will hit ____ the deep freeze.

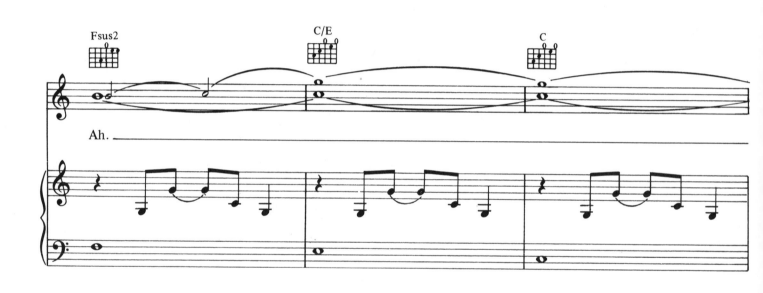

Ah. _____

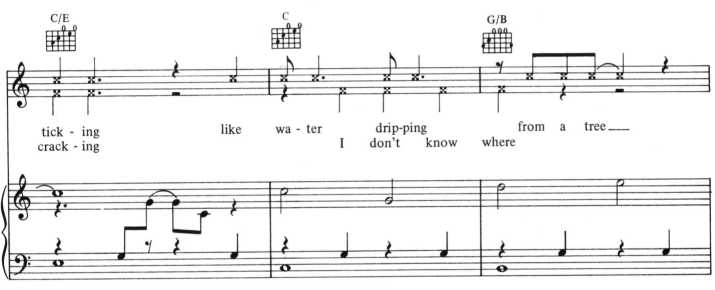

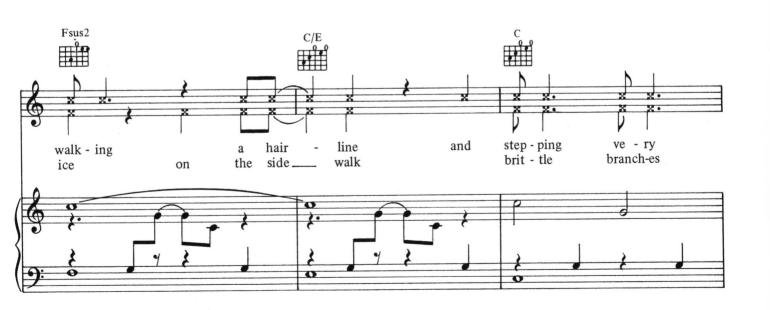

WELCOME TO MY MORNING
(FAREWELL ANDROMEDA)

WORDS & MUSIC BY JOHN DENVER

*Guitarists: Tune sixth string to low D.

think I made it per - fect - ly, I would-n't change a thing. La la la
if the truth is told they will nev - er come a - gain.

To Coda

la la la la la, la la la

1.
la la la la la.

2.
la la la.

71

BIRD ON THE WIRE

WORDS & MUSIC BY LEONARD COHEN

for thee.

And if I _____ if

I've been un - kind. _____ I

hope that you _____ will let it go

by. _____   And if

I _____   if   I've   been   un -

true. _____   I

hope   you   know _____   it   was   nev - er _____   to

you._____ So I

swear by this song_____ I

swear by all I did wrong._____ I will

make it__ I will make it__ all up_____ to

thee.

Like a

free.

Like a bird on the wire
Like a drunk in a midnight choir
I have tried in my way to be free
Like a worm on a hook
Like a knight from some old-fashioned book
I have saved all my ribbons for thee
    If I have been unkind
    I hope that you can just let it go by
    If I have been untrue,
    I hope you know it was never to you.

Like a baby stillborn
Like a beast with his horn
I have torn everyone who reached out for me
But I swear by this song
And by all that I have done wrong
I will make it all up to thee.
    I saw a beggar leaning on his wooden crutch
    He said to me, "You must not ask for so much."
    And a pretty woman leaning in her darkened door,
    She cried to me, "Hey, why not ask for more?"